DIVERSE TEAMS AT WORK

DIVERSE TEAMS AT WORK

Capitalizing on the Power of Diversity

Lee Gardenswartz, PhD

Anita Rowe, PhD

Society for Human Resource Management
Alexandria, Virginia
USA
www.shrm.org

DIVERSE TEAMS AT WORK
Capitalizing on the Power of Diversity

Lee Gardenswartz, Ph.D.
Anita Rowe, Ph.D.

Society for Human Resource Management
Alexandria, Virginia
USA
www.shrm.org

This publication is designed to provide accurate and authoritative information regarding the subject matter covered. It is sold with the understanding that neither the publisher nor the authors is engaged in rendering legal or other professional service. If legal advice or other expert assistance is required, the services of a competent, licensed professional should be sought. The federal and state laws discussed in this book are subject to frequent revision and interpretation by amendments or judicial revisions that may significantly affect employer or employee rights and obligations. Readers are encouraged to seek legal counsel regarding specific policies and practices in their organizations.

This book is published by the Society for Human Resource Management (SHRM©). The interpretations, conclusions, and recommendations in this book are those of the authors and do not necessarily represent those of SHRM.

The Society for Human Resource Management (SHRM) is the world's largest association devoted to human resource management. Representing more than 170,000 individual members, the Society's mission is both to serve human resource management professionals and to advance the profession. Visit SHRM Online at www.shrm.org.

Library of Congress Cataloging-in-Publication Data

Gardenswartz, Lee.
  Diverse teams at work: capitalizing on the power of diversity / Lee Gardenswartz, Anita Rowe.
    p. cm.
  ISBN 1-58644-036-5
  1. Teams in the workplace. 2. Multiculturalism. I. Rowe, Anita, 1946- II. Title.
HD66 .G375 2002
658.4'02—dc21

                                   2002014409

Printed in the United States of America.
10 9 8 7 6 5 4 3 2

Preface

In today's highly competitive world, organizations with downsized staffs and tighter resources are increasingly turning to teams to achieve performance objectives and maximize productivity by solving problems, creating new products, and improving customer service. Often, organizational survival depends on how well those teams work. Yet in today's complex and pluralistic world, where teams are seldom homogeneous, workers often come with different values, norms, languages, and points of view. In such an environment, traditional team building methods, tools, and techniques are not enough.

The concept for *Diverse Teams at Work* began to emerge as we worked in client organizations on two separate yet parallel tracks. First, with the growing focus on teams and employee empowerment, clients were continuing to search for ways to remove obstacles to teamwork and increase the output of work groups. On the other track, changing workforce demographics had radically altered the composition of the employee base, creating work groups made up of people from different generations, genders, races, ethnicities, and life situations.

It became clear to us that instead of remaining separate, the two tracks needed to be integrated. The very work teams that were struggling to become more harmonious, to solve problems, and to implement change were also diverse groups with the whole spectrum of human differences that organizations were training people to deal with in diversity seminars. The potential for creativity, energy, and commitment was waiting to be tapped in these teams.

Diverse Teams at Work brings these two issues together, giving team leaders and members an understanding of what it takes to build an effective team in a diverse environment and providing the methods to do so. It offers both conceptual information about team functioning—the elements of diversity and how they impact one another—as well as practical techniques and tools for intervening in and facilitating team processes to increase group effectiveness.

WHAT THIS BOOK IS AND ISN'T

This book is not about the statistical process measures or analytical problem-solving approaches found in the many excellent quality-improvement books already available. It is rather about the human side of teamwork, especially when those humans are different from one another. The techniques and methods featured here focus on helping teams build common ground, appreciate and capitalize on differences, and overcome the obstacles that diversity sometimes presents.

Perhaps the most important service this book can provide is to help team leaders and members become more flexible and adaptive in the face of an ever-changing economic and social world.

WHAT'S IN THIS BOOK: A CHAPTER-BY-CHAPTER GUIDE

Chapter 1 explains how diverse teams are different from homogeneous ones and dispels some of the myths about diverse teams.

Chapter 2 answers the frequent question, "What is diversity, anyway?" It goes beyond race and gender to include the wide spectrum of differences that make up diversity. The chapter focuses on the four layers of differences—from personality and internal dimensions to external and organizational categories—that impact behavior, assumptions, and opportunities on the job.

Chapter 3 presents a model of team functioning and shows how the diversity of team members can influence each of the four aspects of how teams work.

Chapter 4 gives the reader information about one aspect of teamwork, task focus, and offers processes for defining the team's mission, goals, objectives, and measurement criteria that build common ground.

Chapter 5 looks at another aspect of team functioning, relationships, and provides activities and tools for building strong interpersonal connections and support among diverse co-workers.

Chapter 6 focuses on ways to build teams through structuring interdependence among employees, which requires diverse staff to work together on common goals, projects, and tasks.

Chapter 7 provides a series of group-process interventions that help teams through difficult spots and keep them on track and moving forward.

Chapter 8 gives suggestions for processes to use for teams at different stages and with different needs. From starting new teams and integrating new members to ending group experiences and diagnosing problem spots, the chapter provides answers to the "What do I do now?" question.

Chapter 9 deals not with teams themselves but with their leadership, offering a new model of leadership for today's diverse work groups and organizations.

Chapter 10 concludes the book with a discussion of considerations, challenges, and caveats in building diverse teams.

A compilation of resources for diverse team building is included at the end of the book. It provides an annotated list of books, training activities, and videos about diversity and team building that can be helpful in developing group members and training team leaders.

Lee Gardenswartz
Anita Rowe

Acknowledgments

Our most formidable and important learning experiences involving the building of diverse teams began years ago when we helped the Los Angeles Unified School District work through the stresses, strains, and pains of mandatory integration in 1977. That seminal experience became life changing and set us on a path of helping people in organizations come to understand and find value in the phenomenon of differentness. Through all those years, we have had the benefit of working with many excellent teachers and supporters who helped us gain our experience and hone our skills. One person from those early days stands out: We'd like to thank John E. Jones, Ph.D., our first and best teacher in the field of team building and human dynamics.

We'd also like to thank the following people who have been helpful to us on this particular project:

Judy Rosener, Ph.D., an energetic colleague, friend, and cheerleader who gives us endless support.

Virginia Fleming, Melinda Harris, and Maria Pitts, our typical end users but very atypical, exceptional team leaders, facilitators, and clients who gave us helpful feedback.

Red Badgett and Mihran Sarkesian, whose in-the-trenches reality was our guide.

UCLA Extension Diverse Team Building Class, spring 1993, for bringing their real work issues inside our classroom and laying them at our feet—what a laboratory!

Cindy Zigmund, our editor, and Judy Semler, our agent, who removed the roadblocks so we could write.

Ron Matheson, our right-hand man who not only presents us well on paper but is a constant and dependable source of tangible support.

Our dear friends Francey Gray, Ann Petty, and Sharon Dewees, who generously provided wonderful writing retreats so we could work without interruption or distraction.

Anita's husband Darrell, who continues to show her the richness diversity brings and who reminds her daily that that's why we have chocolate and vanilla.

Beth Ojena, Mark Gardenswartz, Ian Gardenswartz, Jill Ebstein, and Wesley Gardenswartz, siblings who always have (and continue to) teach Lee the beauty and wonder of diversity. You were her first teachers regarding tolerance for and appreciation of differences.

To the executive staff at 1339 Stuart Street, the team builders non-pareil, Rosyne and Nathan Gardenswartz (AKA Lee's parents), Lee wishes she knew their magic or understood how they harnessed such different personalities, talents, skills, and interests to forge the loving and devoted unit they did. They have always been Lee's best team building teachers and role models.